BENEDICT
ARNOLD
FROM PATRIOT TO TRAITOR

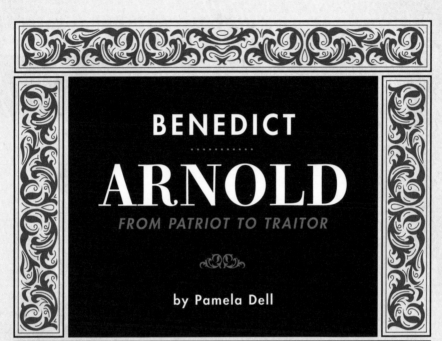

BENEDICT
ARNOLD
FROM PATRIOT TO TRAITOR

by Pamela Dell

Content Adviser: Richard J. Bell,
History Department, Harvard University

Reading Adviser: Rosemary G. Palmer, Ph.D.,
Department of Literacy, College of Education,
Boise State University

COMPASS POINT BOOKS MINNEAPOLIS, MINNESOTA

Compass Point Books
3109 West 50th Street, #115
Minneapolis, MN 55410

Visit Compass Point Books on the Internet at *www.compasspointbooks.com*
or e-mail your request to *custserv@compasspointbooks.com*

Editor: Jill Kalz
Lead Designer: Jaime Martens
Photo Researcher: Svetlana Zhurkina
Page Production: The Design Lab, Bobbie Nuytten
Cartographer: XNR Productions, Inc.
Educational Consultant: Diane Smolinski

Managing Editor: Catherine Neitge
Art Director: Keith Griffin
Production Director: Keith McCormick
Creative Director: Terri Foley

Library of Congress Cataloging-in-Publication Data
Dell, Pamela.
Benedict Arnold : from patriot to traitor / by Pamela Dell.
p. cm. — (Signature lives)
Includes bibliographical references and index.
ISBN 0-7565-0825-8 (hardcover)
1. Arnold, Benedict, 1741–1801—Juvenile literature. 2. American
loyalists—Biography—Juvenile literature. 3. Generals—United States—
Biography—Juvenile literature. 4. United States. Continental Army—
Biography—Juvenile literature. 5. United States—History—Revolution,
1775–1783—Juvenile literature. I. Title. II. Series.
E278.A7D37 2005
973.3'092—dc22   2004023196

Signature Lives

REVOLUTIONARY WAR ERA

The American Revolution created heroes—and traitors—
who shaped the birth of a new nation: the United States
of America. "Taxation without representation" was a serious
problem for the American colonies during the late 1700s.
Great Britain imposed harsh taxes and didn't give the
colonists a voice in their own government. The colonists
rebelled and declared their independence from Britain—
the war was on.

Benedict Arnold

Table of Contents

1 RECKLESS BOY

Chapter

❧❦❧

In the mid-1700s in the bustling town of Norwich, Connecticut, everyone knew who the biggest daredevil was. It was that kid who took running leaps over loaded wagons. It was the one who climbed the masts of sailing vessels on the wharf, then scrambled down and raced off before anyone could catch him. It was that reckless boy who talked his friends into stealing barrels of tar from the shipyard one night to light the most spectacular bonfire anyone had ever seen.

The only thing that ruined that prank was the town police officer. Every boy involved ran the minute he saw the officer coming—all but one. The daredevil kid stood his ground. In fact, he was outraged that a pudgy old man had put an end to his

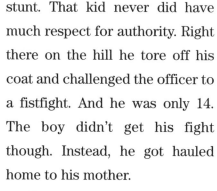

> *Even as an adult, when in grave danger Arnold seemed to have confidence in his own safety. To his sister Hannah he once wrote, "That Providence which has carried me through so many dangers is still my protection. I am in the way of my duty and know no fear."*

stunt. That kid never did have much respect for authority. Right there on the hill he tore off his coat and challenged the officer to a fistfight. And he was only 14. The boy didn't get his fight though. Instead, he got hauled home to his mother.

But perhaps the most memorable trick he pulled was at the town mill. With onlookers egging him on, he managed to catch hold of one of the blades of the revolving waterwheel. He clung to the blade as it carried him high then brought him down again, plunging him beneath the water. He surfaced a moment later, still clinging to the blade and laughing like a demon. Finally, when he was at the highest point again, he let go. He dropped, splashed into the water, and swam for shore, not a scratch on him. The kid was always trying to prove himself in one way or another.

People in town knew who was responsible for these pranks. It was that kid whose family had once been one of the most successful and respected in all of Norwich—before his father became an embarrassing drunk. It was the kid who would grow up to be a military genius of the Revolutionary War, then throw it all away. It was the kid who by the end of

his life would be branded a traitor, a turncoat, a spy against the patriot cause. Everyone knew his name well. They still do.

At the age of 39, Benedict Arnold was a wanted man for betraying his country.

That kid was Benedict Arnold. ✇

2 A Start in the World

⚬◦⟨∞⟩◦⚬

It was the second week of January 1741 and Benedict Arnold IV was anxious. His wife, Hannah, was soon to give birth. Mr. Arnold wanted a son, one who would grow up to join his successful merchant-trading business. Perhaps he might contribute great things as a leader in government, just as his great-great-grandfather had done. That ancestor, Benedict Arnold I, had become a wealthy landholder and governor of Rhode Island colony.

Through the generations the Arnold name had maintained its respected status in the colonies. By Puritan custom, the firstborn boy and girl in a family were usually named after their parents. So, in the Arnold family, the name "Benedict" was passed down too. But the first Benedict's vast fortune dwindled as

Like the apothecary pictured here, Benedict Arnold V made medicines by grinding the ingredients with a club-shaped stick called a pestle against the sides of a bowl called a mortar.

*The birthplace
of Benedict
Arnold, in
Norwich,
Connecticut, as
it appeared
circa 1880*

it was divided among many heirs and descendants. By the time Benedict IV, the daredevil's father, was born, there was no wealth and no land for him.

Knowing he had to make his own fortune, the young Benedict IV chose Norwich, Connecticut, as a good place to settle down. Norwich sat 12 miles (19 kilometers) inland from the Atlantic Ocean at the point where the Thames River split into two smaller rivers. There, he and his brother began apprenticeships as coopers, or barrel makers.

By the 1700s, with its excellent location,

Norwich was a growing center of shipbuilding and trade. Great sailing ships took goods such as cattle and cotton to Canada, England, and the West Indies. They came back loaded with fine silks, molasses, medicines, and spices. Benedict IV quickly saw that he could acquire a much greater fortune as a merchant than he could as a cooper. Slowly he began to build his fortunes.

In November 1732, Benedict IV married a wealthy widow, Hannah Waterman King. This marriage instantly put Benedict into the highest level of Norwich society. And on January 14, 1741, Benedict IV got his wish: Hannah gave birth to a son, Benedict V. In the following years, the Arnolds had four more children, named Hannah, Mary, Absalom King, and Elizabeth.

Benedict V was an exceptional child, and a prankster of the most notorious sort. He had dark hair and a strong, athletic build. He was also highly intelligent and usually wild and willful in his quest to prove himself.

Growing up in Norwich, Benedict ran free throughout the town. He swam in the rivers and fished for eels and mackerel. He

> *"Benedict" was an unusual name when Benedict Arnold V was born. Most colonial children were given names from the Bible. His name came from the Latin word Benedictus, meaning "blessing." The surname "Arnold" means "the eagle's power" in the ancient German language from which it originates.*

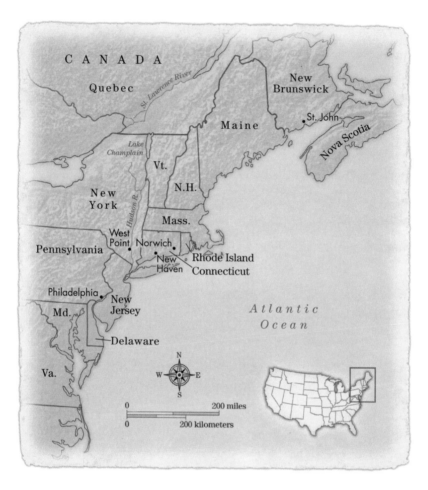

Benedict Arnold spent much of his life in the northeastern United States.

learned to hunt, trap, canoe, ride horses, and ice skate. Benedict went on trading voyages with his father, who had acquired many ships. They sailed to places as far away as the West Indies on trading expeditions.

Onboard his father's ships, Benedict learned to sail and navigate the ocean. He loved life at sea. It inflamed his keen sense of adventure. It also soothed his fiery soul. Onboard a sailing vessel, with the seabirds wheeling above and the endless cycle of sun and then storm clouds, Benedict was free.

In the autumn of 1750, the younger Arnold son, Absalom King, passed away, leaving Benedict as the sole surviving male heir. Benedict's parents wanted to give him every advantage, including an excellent education. In 1752, they enrolled him in the private boarding school of the Reverend James Cogswell. Cogswell was a well-respected minister and a learned scholar. He was also a graduate of the prestigious Yale College in New Haven, Connecticut. He specialized in the education of boys whose fathers were "gentlemen of trade."

Being taught by Reverend Cogswell provided students with many privileges, including access to universities such as Yale. But being a good student was not enough. Students also had to behave. When Benedict first entered Cogswell's school, Mrs. Arnold wrote to the reverend and encouraged him to use whatever means necessary to discipline her son:

> *It is with a great deal of satisfaction that I commit my uncultivated child to your care under God. Pray don't spare ye rod and spoil ye child ... If you should find him backward and unteachable, pray don't be soon discouraged but use all possible means, again and again.*

At school, in Reverend Cogswell's home, Benedict studied mathematics, logic, Greek, Latin, public speaking, the Bible, history, and English. At night he slept with the other students in a dorm-like attic room at the top of the house.

Benedict may have done his best to behave. But on occasion, even at school, he could not resist a death-defying stunt. Reverend Cogswell once wrote a concerned letter to Mrs. Arnold about a terrible fire that had broken out in a local building. Benedict had neither set the fire nor helped to put it out, but he was spotted atop the roof of the burning building. While a horrified crowd looked on, Benedict made his way along the topmost roof beam. Like a born tightrope walker, he moved forward with arms out-

Yale College was founded in 1701 by Connecticut Presbyterian ministers.

stretched, flames leaping up all around him. Somehow he made it off the building safely.

Benedict had his fun, but he also applied himself to his studies. His mother wrote affectionate letters and even sent gifts of chocolate and money. But throughout the summer of 1753, most of her news from home was bad.

That year, a killer disease called diphtheria swept through Norwich. In the fall, the disease took Benedict's youngest sisters, 8-year-old Mary and 3-year-old Elizabeth, one just 19 days after the other. Only his sister Hannah survived. Being away at school may have saved Benedict's life.

Death was not the only trouble with which the Arnolds were coping. Captain Arnold's business was heavily in debt and doing poorly. Benedict's father began to drink heavily. By the spring of 1755, Benedict's education became an expense his family could not afford. At only 14 years old he was called home.

Back in Norwich, Benedict saw how bad things really were. With his business gone, Captain Arnold now spent most of his time drunk in the local bars. It was a humiliation Benedict could barely endure. He had left for school as an elite member of society, but he returned home to disgrace.

Disgrace seemed to spark in the boy a burning need to achieve wealth, fame, and a solid standing in high society so that no one could sneer at him again. His mother was the first to help Benedict build the security he so desperately craved.

In 1755, Benedict became the apprentice of Hannah Arnold's cousins, Joshua and Daniel Lathrop. The Lathrops had a thriving apothecary business as well as a lively trade in general merchandise. They imported goods from Canada, Europe, and the West Indies. They sold everything from potions and medicines to books, fabrics, perfumes, and wines.

As an apprentice, Benedict would essentially be their servant for seven years. During that time he would learn everything about their business. Then, at the age of 21, he would be free to build his own business.

Benedict immediately began to thrive under this arrangement. Daniel Lathrop and his wife lived in an impressive riverside mansion. Residing with them, Benedict enjoyed the elegant surroundings and the beautiful gardens. He soon grew accustomed to having servants and slaves to care for his every need.

For the next seven years Benedict worked hard. His intelligence, energy, and superior attention to detail won him more and more responsibility. Before he was 20, the Lathrops had put their nephew in charge of buying and selling cargo far from Norwich. They had sent him alone on many sea

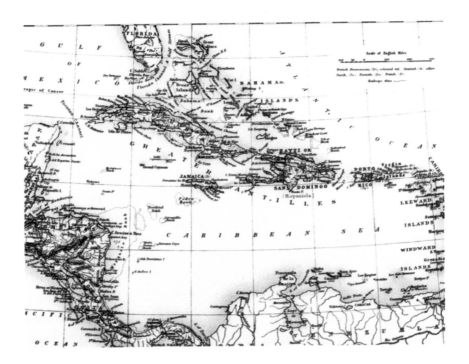

voyages to places as distant as the Caribbean and the West Indies.

The West Indies is a collection of islands that lies between North America and South America.

Then, in 1759, Benedict's mother, Hannah, died, and his father's drinking problem spun entirely out of control. Captain Arnold was arrested for a disruptive display of public drunkenness. Benedict seethed with disgust as he bailed his father out of jail. He wanted to get out of the town where his family's shame reflected badly on himself.

In 1761, a year before Benedict left the Lathrops, Captain Arnold died, broken and grief-stricken. Benedict and his sister Hannah were orphans with no inheritance at all. Even the house they had grown up in was not theirs. Creditors had taken ownership of it to pay off the late Captain Arnold's remaining debts. Now it was time for Benedict to make his own way in the world.

New Haven, Connecticut, was said to be the most beautiful town in New England in the mid-1700s. At its center was a large green park, bordered by lush trees, Yale College, and three churches with spires reaching to the sky. Beyond town were rolling hills and farmlands as far as one could see.

The city's deep harbor opened into Long Island Sound, making it a lively center of seagoing trade. Ships came from and sailed to New York, Boston, Canada, and far beyond. Population growth in New Haven was explosive. Altogether, it was an ideal place for a young man starting out in the apothecary-merchant business.

In 1762, Benedict opened a small shop on Chapel Street. He used everything he had learned from the Lathrops to create a shop unlike any other. Instead of being just a simple apothecary, it was more like a small department store.

Benedict Arnold, druggist and bookseller, did well. By 1765, he had relocated his business to larger quarters overlooking the harbor. He owned three ships and had repaid his debt to the Lathrops. Also, he had brought his sister from Norwich to New Haven to help oversee the business. With Hannah

there, Benedict could afford to be away for months. From spring until fall he was at sea, carrying horses, lumber, furs, and cotton to the faraway ports he had traveled to nearly all his life. He returned with necessities and exotic goods to fill his shop. At the same time that Benedict was building his business, however, forces were at work to tear it down. ℘

Women apothe-caries were extremely rare in the United States until well into the 1800s.

3 REBELS RISING

Chapter

୬୦୦୨୧

In 1754, the year Arnold turned 13, the French and Indian War broke out in North America between the French, their Native American allies, and the British over North American land rights. The conflict spread to other parts of the world as Britain struggled to enlarge its empire. In 1763, the Treaty of Paris officially ended the war. But nine years of conflict had left the English Empire with a huge debt. Now the young new king of England, George III, decided that the American colonists would help pay that debt.

Tax laws, established by the British, had long been in place to regulate colonial trade but were rarely enforced. In 1764, drastic changes began to occur. That year the Sugar Act came into effect.

The high cost of providing weapons, uniforms, and wages during the French and Indian War put great financial pressure on the British Empire.

Under the Sugar Act, traders had to pay taxes on molasses, imported wines and sugars of all kinds, and on many non-sugar products as well, such as indigo, textiles, and coffee beans.

The following year, the Stamp Act imposed a tax on all paper documents, including newspapers, land deeds, stationery, diplomas, and much more. To avoid paying these taxes, the colonists resorted to smuggling. They always had. The colonial tax inspectors often ignored what they saw. But now, for the first time ever, British inspectors were stationed in New England ports to check every ship's freight for taxable goods.

Many colonists had no desire to help pay for Britain's empire-building. The traders knew that if they had to pay the enormous multiple taxes, they would be run out of business. The colonies depended on the lively commerce generated by the traders. In every way, colonial economy would suffer greatly if taxation were upheld. The general attitude in the colonies was that smuggling was not wrong. It was essential to keep business alive. And like most other traders, Benedict Arnold engaged in it.

British tax laws sunk colonial America into an economic depression even as smuggling continued. Arnold had both bought extensively on credit and had also extended much credit. With creditors hounding him, he in turn hounded those in debt to him. By 1767 he was close to ruin. His greatest fear was following in his father's footsteps. But Arnold was a fighter. He aggressively defended himself against lawsuits and challenged anyone who tried to damage his business or reputation. After weathering many ups and downs, he was back on top.

By 1770, not yet 30, he was again one of the wealthiest and most successful merchants in New Haven, Connecticut. Also by then, he was a married man with two sons. Arnold had married 22-year-old Margaret Mansfield, the daughter of a county sheriff, in February of 1767. Their firstborn son, Benedict VI, was born the following February, and their second son, Richard, was born in 1769. The Arnold home was an impressive mansion, and the family traveled in its own fancy coach. The former rebel felt a smug satisfaction at all he had achieved. The future looked promising once again.

But Arnold could not forget how his business had suffered as a result of British trade laws. His loyalty to the British king dwindled.

Arnold was not the only one feeling defiant. Unrest had been mounting throughout the colonies since the Sugar Act was imposed. Over the years, the protests had become increasingly violent. But most colonists still saw themselves as loyal British subjects. As such, they felt entitled to the unspoken, "natural" rights of all British subjects: the rights to life, liberty, and the ownership of property. The king's tax laws threatened all three of these.

By 1770, the only tax that remained in place was the Tea Act. That law made British tea less expensive than the tea sold by New Englanders. Great Britain expected the colonists to buy its cheaper tea, but colonists refused. In Boston in December 1773, a group of the most radical rebels threw an entire cargo of British tea overboard one night. This

protest, known as the Boston Tea Party, brought more repression against the colonists. The following year, along with hundreds of others, Arnold was fully swept up by the frenzy to get rid of the British. He had become a patriot rebel.

Some men disguised themselves as Native Americans to avoid being recognized and later punished for their roles in the Boston Tea Party.

Arnold saw himself not simply as a follower. No, he would be at the forefront of the fight, a heralded

Rebels threw 342 chests of British tea into Boston harbor.

military leader. He would be the man forever remembered for driving the British out.

By 1775, thousands who had once considered themselves the king's loyal subjects were taking another view. And Arnold had begun his climb to military glory as captain of the Governor's Second Company of Foot Guards, a New Haven company of 65 "gentlemen of influence and high respectability." From December of 1774 until the spring of 1775, he had done his best to turn them into a polished military regiment.

Now, in April 1775, the Foot Guards were en route to join thousands of other colonists in Cambridge, Massachusetts—the command center of the colonial resistance. British soldiers, or redcoats, were swarming the colonies, and the colonial militia was mounting a resistance. The most radical members of the resistance, men like Samuel Adams and John Hancock, intended to fight until freedom from British rule was accomplished.

The road to Cambridge was long and dusty. But as captain of his regiment, Arnold barely noticed. He was full of pride and military ambition. His troops were a striking bunch. They wore uniforms that included scarlet coats with silver buttons, fancy

Arnold's first attempt at serving in the military was disappointing. In 1757, a frantic call had gone out for colonial troops when French and Indian soldiers attacked Massachusetts. Arnold was 16 at the time and still working for the Lathrops. But they had given him permission to march north. Before Arnold reached the battleground, however, the conflict ended, unfavorably for the British. The French had gained control of Fort William Henry on New York's Lake George. Arnold returned home with no exciting tales of war to tell.

Arnold was promoted to colonel before the raid on Ticonderoga.

ruffled shirts, and dark breeches. They were also well trained and disciplined. Including Arnold himself, they had each paid three dollars each a week to learn military drills from an expert.

On the morning of April 22, 1775, Arnold's troops gathered on New Haven's village green to begin their march for Cambridge. But they needed guns and ammunition stored in the town "powder house." New Haven's town council was not in favor of the colonists' resistance, however. They refused to open the storehouse.

But Arnold was not about to take no for an answer. "None but Almighty God shall prevent my marching!" Arnold is said to have bellowed. He demanded the storehouse keys, threatening that he and his men would simply break in and take what they needed if the council did not comply. Arnold got what he wanted. The storehouse was quickly unlocked. The Foot Guards grabbed weapons and ammunition and marched out of town.

Along the way, Arnold heard that the patriot militia was desperately in need of ammunition, muskets, and especially cannons. From his wide travels as a trader, Arnold knew the northern terrain and the British-held forts well. More importantly, he knew where ammunition was being held.

Fort Ticonderoga rose in his mind. ॐ

Chapter

4 TAKING TICONDEROGA

❧⸲⸲❧

Fort Ticonderoga sat at the south end of Lake Champlain in New York. There, and farther south at Crown Point, Arnold knew plenty of weapons were stored. He also knew that both forts were miserably rundown and that few British troops were stationed in either place. He imagined how easy it would be for a few hundred eager patriots to attack and come away with the needed weapons. If a real war broke out, being in control of these forts would be a big advantage for the patriots. This was Arnold's chance to prove himself as a military leader.

When he reached Cambridge, Massachusetts, Arnold immediately met with the Massachusetts Committee of Safety, which was in charge of many government and military duties. He told them about

Ethan Allen led the troops during the successful raid on Fort Ticonderoga in 1775 but gave Benedict Arnold the honor of co-commanding.

Today, Ethan Allen is considered a folk hero in Vermont for fiercely defending the rights of landowners in the state when it was known as the New Hampshire Grants.

the weapons at Ticonderoga. Arnold proposed an attack on the well-stocked fort, which he offered to lead. After some hesitation, the committee accepted his proposal. They promoted Arnold to the rank of colonel in the Massachusetts militia and promised to give him whatever he needed to get the job done. Thrilled to be put in charge of this important mission, Arnold quickly organized and set off. But just as he reached the Massachusetts border, he received news that threw him into furious action. The Green Mountain Boys, led by Ethan Allen, were also planning a Ticonderoga raid.

The "Boys" were a rough band of land speculators from the New Hampshire Grants (later known as Vermont). They had been branded outlaws because of the violent tactics they used to keep New Yorkers from moving in on their territory. Arnold learned that the Boys were already gathered only a few miles from the fort.

Arnold had no experience in battle. But he had wits, drive, and a lack of fear. Most importantly, he had official orders. No one was going to rob him of his chance to perform. Arnold had commanded his assistants to recruit as many troops as possible and meet him in the Hampshire Grants. Now he jumped on his horse and galloped north at top speed.

Arnold caught up with the Green Mountain Boys in a rustic tavern in the village of Castleton. He showed them his orders and brashly announced that the Ticonderoga raid was officially under his command. But to the Boys, a pompous man in a fancy scarlet jacket claiming authority was a joke. Scoffing at Arnold's papers, they made their own announcement. They would go to Ticonderoga only under the leadership of Ethan Allen, or they would pack up and go home.

Arnold quickly met with Allen, who had no official orders whatsoever. When Allen realized that Arnold was an officer sent by the committee, he agreed to share command. A joint command was hardly the scenario Arnold had imagined for himself. But his own troops still had not arrived. Allen was going to strike the fort with or without him. If he didn't agree to the terms, he would most definitely be left behind.

Arnold was so frantic to catch up with the Green Mountain Boys that he nearly rode his horse to death. After 15 miles (24 km) over muddy, mountainous terrain, the horse was ruined. Arnold later billed the Massachusetts Provincial Congress 16 pounds for it. Congress agreed to give him three pounds.

The British surrendered Fort Ticonderoga without a fight.

Allen planned to slip across the waters of Lake Champlain under cover of night, scale the cliffs, and charge with nearly 300 men before morning.

In the pre-dawn hours of May 10, 1775, in the midst of a violent rainstorm, the plan went into effect. As dawn approached, however, only about 80 men had made it across to the inlet below the fort. Arnold and Allen felt they could not wait any longer. They chose to go ahead without the others.

As Arnold had predicted, few troops were stationed at Ticonderoga. Everyone at the fort was taken completely by surprise. The commanding officer, Captain William Delaplace, seeing no way out, quickly surrendered the fort. In the following days, Crown Point was taken as well, in another Green Mountain escapade.

On May 18, Arnold made one more daring mission—this time with his own men. Without being given authority to do so, he sailed to St. Johns at the far north end of Lake Champlain in Canada. There he outwitted the British on their turf and captured an important warship. Without the ship, the enemy's ability to transport troops and supplies would be ruined. Arnold's bold move was significant for another reason as well. It was the first time in history that a foreign country was successfully invaded by Americans.

But Arnold's style had made him bitter enemies among the Green Mountain Boys. Some of them had made reports against him to the Second Continental Congress in Philadelphia and to the Massachusetts Provincial Congress. Despite Arnold's heroism and professionalism at both Ticonderoga and St. Johns,

British warships ruled the waters of Lake Champlain until the late 18th century.

Ethan Allen ended up with most of the credit.

Many in Congress appreciated Arnold's value in holding and running the fort. But some had serious misgivings about his impulsive tendencies. They worried that further aggressive acts by the patriots might prevent patching things up with Great Britain. And reconciliation was still the aim of many. Arnold might be dangerous to that aim if he remained in command.

Another factor was at work as well. No central military authority had yet been established among the colonies to give them unity. Each colony was responsible for its own organization of troops, funding, and military operations. Getting any coop-

eration among different bands of revolutionary rebels was difficult. Most of the revolutionaries understood this. But Arnold did not. He did not have the gifts of a politician. He had no understanding of how to work well with those in power to benefit himself. All he knew was the desperate need to defend his honor and not relive the shame he had felt as a boy. These were the fatal flaws that drove him. ❧

5 THE TREK TO QUEBEC

In mid-June 1775, Congress abruptly demoted Arnold to second in command at Fort Ticonderoga, and Colonel Benjamin Hinman of Connecticut was put in charge. Arnold was stunned.

The change in command was a practical compromise. Arnold was a commanding officer from Massachusetts. Because Connecticut had more troops, Massachusetts had agreed to Connecticut's control of the region. But Arnold did not see any justice in this. After all his achievements in Champlain, he felt it was a personal insult of the highest order.

To add insult to injury, the Massachusetts committee was questioning the expenses Arnold had claimed for overseeing Fort Ticonderoga. Arnold

Arnold's invasion of Quebec took him on a harrowing journey over land and sea.

had spent generously out of his own pocket to cover the needs of the fort and his troops, but he lacked receipts for all the claimed expenses. Angry that anyone would question his abilities or his honesty, Arnold resigned.

Discouraged and disgusted, Arnold journeyed home to New Haven in mid-July. But bad news reached him before he arrived. His young wife, Margaret, had unexpectedly died. Arnold's sister Hannah assumed the care for his sons.

At home, Arnold was struck with a case of gout, a severe inflammation of the joints. He was bedridden for several weeks, but his mind would not rest. He formed a plan to firmly secure the colonists' hold on Lake Champlain. He would offer to lead a raid against Quebec and Montreal in Canada.

Many others had also talked about an attack on Canada. By the summer of 1775, Congress had finally chosen George Washington as commander in chief of the Continental Army. Washington wanted to hit Canada from two directions at once. The main body of troops would go up Lake Champlain and the St. Lawrence River to take Montreal. The other would burrow through the Maine wilderness to invade Quebec City. Arnold knew this second job was made for him.

Recovered from his illness, Arnold traveled to Cambridge, Massachusetts, in August to meet with General Washington. Washington liked Arnold immediately, and with Washington's approval, Congress gave Arnold command of this second arm of the invasion. Arnold assured Washington that he could reach Quebec within about three weeks.

On September 19, 1775, Arnold set sail from Newburyport, Massachusetts, with just over 1,000 troops. There were four skilled guides and about 300 rough and ready frontiersmen led by Captain Daniel Morgan, an experienced soldier.

Arnold had ordered 200 flat-bottomed boats for the journey. But the boats had been hastily made. They leaked badly, ruining supplies, soaking the men, and causing food to rot. The troops encountered rapids, raging currents, and twisting, turning courses. When walking on land, they were forced to hack their way through dense forest. Mucky, root-infested ground shredded their shoes to nothing and left their feet bare and bloody.

Colonial troops crossed the St. Lawrence River in 1775 to attack Quebec.

Soon the weather worsened. Freezing rainstorms drenched everything. Rivers swelled and became even more dangerous. After weeks of rain, snow set in. Men grew sick and had little to eat besides soggy flour. Able to endure no more, about 300 troops at the rear of the march deserted, taking much of the remaining food and supplies with them.

Desperate for food, the remaining troops began boiling rawhide and drinking the resulting juice. They boiled and ate anything they had: moccasin leather, shaving soap, even candles, which were made from animal fat and did provide some nourishment. Finally the men were forced to kill and eat their dogs.

Through all of these hardships, Arnold never wavered in his courage and confidence. He searched for supplies and did everything he could to boost his men's morale. His attention to their needs and his unbreakable spirit gave them courage to press on to Canada.

In early November, Arnold and his men stumbled out of the woods at the banks of the St. Lawrence River. The trek had taken twice as long as expected, but it was one of the most outstanding military feats in early U.S. history.

Quebec was just across the river. Arnold knew seizing control of the fort there would be difficult with so few men. But U.S. general Richard Montgomery had successfully taken Montreal. Now, on December 2, 1775, he and his troops joined Arnold outside Quebec.

Arnold's journey through the Maine wilderness did not include only men. At least two wives of Pennsylvania frontiersmen refused to be left behind. One was the wife of a private who fell seriously ill far into the journey and could not continue. For the sake of survival, the private's regiment was forced to move on. But his wife stayed with him until he died. Having no shovel to dig a grave, she covered him in leaves, picked up his gun, and hurried to catch up with the rest of the troops. They had already traveled 20 miles (32 km) when she reached them.

The British had about 1,200 men stationed in Quebec. Arnold's and Montgomery's troops barely numbered 900. The leaders decided their best chance would be to attack in a blizzard. All they had to do was wait for one to blow in. As fortune would have it, a blinding snowstorm came their way on New Year's Eve.

Montgomery's column charged the fort on one side. But Montgomery was killed almost immediately by enemy fire. On the opposite side, Arnold's troops were trapped in the narrow lanes outside the fort. Many were killed in the crossfire, and half of Arnold's troops were taken prisoner. Musket shot pierced Arnold's left leg, badly wounding him, but he did not quit the battle immediately. Leaning against a wall as the storm raged around him, he shouted orders. Finally, weakened by serious blood loss, he was carried to a makeshift hospital.

Despite this setback, Arnold managed to maintain his siege against Quebec into the spring of 1776. With the thaw, however, enemy reinforcement troops began arriving by water, led by British commander General Guy Carleton.

Far outnumbered, the patriots under Arnold's command had nevertheless shown remarkable strength. For his courage and leadership, Congress promoted Arnold to brigadier general. When the Americans left Canada, Arnold waited until all his troops had set sail down Lake Champlain to safer ground. Only then did he board the last ship, the final patriot to leave Canada. ॐ

Chapter

6 VALIANT ACTION, MOUNTING WOES

❧❧❧

Despite Arnold's heroic efforts, the opportunity to seize control of the Canadian forts had slipped away. He knew what was coming next: the battle for control of Lake Champlain. The redcoats would be heading south from Canada, hoping to retake Ticonderoga and Crown Point. At the same time, enemy troops already in America would attempt to capture New York. If successful, this two-part strategy would cut off the eastern colonies—all of New England—from the rest of America. The patriot rebellion would be stopped in its tracks.

Arnold threw himself into planning a defense. He got approval to assemble a fleet of boats. He wrote letters listing what he needed in terms of weapons, ammunition, and recruits. He trained men to sail,

On October 11, 1776, a British force of some 30 warships carrying nearly 700 seamen set sail on Lake Champlain to destroy Arnold's tiny patriot fleet.

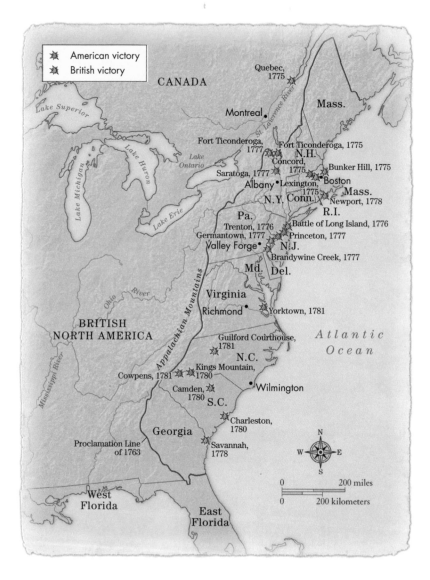

American victory

British victory

CANADA

Quebec, 1775

Mass.

Montreal

Lake Superior

Lake Huron

Lake Michigan

Lake Ontario

Lake Erie

Fort Ticonderoga, 1777

Fort Ticonderoga, 1775

N.H.

Concord, 1775

Bunker Hill, 1775

Saratoga, 1777

Albany

Lexington, 1775

Boston

N.Y. Conn.

Mass.

Newport, 1778

R.I.

Pa.

Battle of Long Island, 1776

Trenton, 1776

Germantown, 1777

Princeton, 1777

Valley Forge

N.J.

Brandywine Creek, 1777

Md. Del.

Ohio River

Virginia

Richmond

Yorktown, 1781

Appalachian Mountains

BRITISH NORTH AMERICA

Atlantic Ocean

Guilford Courthouse, 1781

N.C.

Kings Mountain, 1780

Cowpens, 1781

Camden, 1780

Wilmington

S.C.

Charleston, 1780

Mississippi River

Georgia

Proclamation Line of 1763

Savannah, 1778

West Florida

East Florida

N W E S

0   200 miles

0   200 kilometers

Major battles of the Revolution were fought throughout the colonies.

including many who had never been on a boat.

In September 1776, Arnold learned that the British had a monstrous prize. Named the *Inflexible*, it was a three-masted, 80-foot-long (24-meter) warship that carried 20 cannons. Nothing the patriots had could possibly compete.

Arnold decided to position his fleet in a channel between Valcour Island and the western shore of Lake Champlain. If the British wanted to come for the patriots, they would need to send their ships through the narrow channel one at a time, reducing the force with which they could attack.

Weeks passed. Then, on the misty gray morning of October 11, 1776, patriot scouts sounded a gun blast of warning. A long line of British ships appeared on the horizon. The *Inflexible* was in the lead. Arnold's fleet included only about 15 ships.

The enemy sailed just past the southern end of Valcour Island and then came back between the island and the mainland. This cut off Arnold's escape route south to Ticonderoga. But because of unfavorable winds, the *Inflexible* was not within fighting range. The British had only managed to get 17 of their own ships into position.

Furious fighting raged for seven hours. Arnold moved like a demon across his ship's deck as the guns blazed all around. As night fell, the *Inflexible* finally regained her sail and moved in to join the other ships. But darkness brought the battle to a halt.

That night a shroud of heavy fog fell over the lake. Arnold knew his troops could not last another day of similar fighting, especially with the huge

The patriots fought in the Battle of Valcour Island using wooden gunboats similar to this replica.

British battleship against them. But the daredevil boy was lurking within the man that night.

Arnold ordered his ships to pull anchor. All lights were extinguished, and no one spoke. The rebels sailed silently forward, single file in the dark. One by one, they slipped undetected between the British ships. Arnold's ship passed by last.

As soon as every intact ship was safely past the British line, the patriots raced southward. At dawn, the enemy discovered the tactic and gave chase. Another vicious battle occurred as the Americans rushed toward Fort Ticonderoga. When they finally pulled to shore, Arnold set fire to every ship in his fleet that had not been destroyed. This would prevent the British from using them. American flags flew high as the ships burned, signifying they had not been captured.

Arnold and about 200 other survivors traveled to Fort Crown Point on foot. As Arnold had hoped, the British retreated back to Canada. Another winter was coming, and Lake Champlain would soon be frozen over. The fight would not resume until spring.

But Arnold's many enemies refused to credit him for what he had accomplished—keeping Lake Champlain from falling back to the British. Rather, they accused him of fleeing like a coward and then destroying a small but valuable fleet of American warships.

Discouraged, Arnold returned to New England for the winter. Then in February 1777, Congress bypassed him and promoted five other brigadier generals to the rank of major general. All five were below Arnold in seniority, and none of them had the outstanding service record that Arnold had.

Arnold was not the only one outraged by this

obvious slap in the face. General Washington was equally appalled. He urged Congress to promote Arnold as well. They refused.

The summer before, Arnold had listened to the reading of the Declaration of Independence. But as he fought for independence, the assaults against him seemed never-ending. Was the fight for liberty really worth his sacrifices? How successful would the struggle be when military promotions were given to those he considered incompetent instead of to those who merited it?

George Washington accepted the surrender of British general Cornwalis in 1781, bringing the Revolutionary War to an end.

Arnold felt his only honorable course was to resign until a formal inquiry could be made and his name cleared. But before he took that action, battle called him again.

In April 1777, news came that about 4,000 British troops were moving toward Danbury, Connecticut. Danbury was the site of a large patriot arsenal. The redcoats needed the weapons and ammunition. They wanted to destroy the town in a show of force.

Together Arnold and General David Wooster

enlisted as many local militiamen as they could. With only about 600 troops, they rushed to Danbury's defense. But they were too late and too few in number. Danbury had burned to the ground.

Nevertheless, Arnold and Wooster made a furious attack upon the retreating British troops. General Wooster was seriously wounded and died a few days later. Seriously outnumbered, Arnold's troops panicked and fled. Their desperate commander rode wildly back and forth between them and the enemy, a one-man rear guard.

One of Arnold's worst enemies was a Massachusetts lawyer named John Brown. In 1777 Brown publicly attacked Arnold's character, claiming, "Money is this man's God and to get enough of it, he would sacrifice his country." Further, Brown claimed Arnold had stolen military property while in Canada and demanded Arnold's arrest.

Musket balls flew furiously all around him. Two horses, one after another, were shot from under him. Arnold's heroic action at the Danbury battle finally paid off. Congress promoted him to major general. Arnold was not satisfied, however. Those who had received the earlier promotions were still his seniors in rank.

Congress was also questioning his Canadian campaign expenses. That they would question him was an insult of the worst kind. Arnold began to contemplate resigning again. ℘

7 LOST GLORY AT SARATOGA

Chapter

❧❦❧

Benedict Arnold was first and foremost a man of action. Resignation did not suit him. Before he could return to civilian life, he was back in the fray. Fort Ticonderoga had again fallen to the British. Now, in 1777, the enemy was approaching Albany, New York. Led by General John Burgoyne, they planned to take control of the entire Mohawk Valley and crush the rebellion in the northeast.

By August, the British had three forces moving toward Albany. One, led by Lieutenant Colonel Barry St. Leger, was marching toward American-held Fort Stanwix. Arnold volunteered to go in and stop them. St. Leger's troops far outnumbered Arnold's, but Arnold's cunning outfoxed them.

Arnold's reputation was by then well known to the

Even with his horse shot out from under him, Benedict Arnold bravely continued to fend off the British in the Battle of Saratoga in 1777.

Born in England in 1727, Horatio Gates served with the British army during the French and Indian War but fought with the patriots once the Revolution broke out.

redcoats and their Indian allies. In a strategic move, he sent two men ahead of his troops to spread the rumor that General Arnold was moving full speed toward them, along with a massive army.

This bit of tactical brilliance paid off. The news struck terror in the Indian troops. They fled. Their fear spread to the British troops as well. They ran too, leaving every bit of their equipment and supplies behind—which Arnold's men took full advantage of.

After this victory, Arnold was called to northern military headquarters near Saratoga, New York. There he came under the direct command of an old acquaintance, General Horatio Gates.

These two men could not have been more different. Arnold was brash, restless, and impatient. His style was to take the offensive and strike wherever there was opportunity. Gates was middle-aged, slow, and cautious to the extreme. Some soldiers even referred to him as "Granny Gates." He relied on defensive tactics and had none of Arnold's innate brilliance as a military planner.

Gates had positioned his armies at Bemis Heights, a high bluff overlooking the Hudson River. From this vantage point he would have a good view of Burgoyne's troops as they approached along the river. His plan was to wait there until the British attacked, rather than initiate combat himself.

Arnold bristled. The idea of simply sitting there and waiting to be attacked was absurd to him. Rather, Arnold envisioned a powerful offensive that would destroy Burgoyne's troops. Perhaps, under his leadership, it would even be the final showdown between Britain and the United States. The value of his contribution would then be undeniable.

The man Arnold asked to go before his troops with the rumor of doom was Hon Yost Schuyler. Appearing to be crazy, Hon Yost rushed into St. Leger's encampment, eyes wild and terrified. When asked how many men Arnold had with him, the man gestured to the trees, as if to say "as many as there are leaves." With perfect timing, the Oneida Indian Arnold had sent with Hon Yost to watch over him then appeared. He also looked frantic and backed up Hon Yost's story. The entire camp fled in terror.

But even as the British army drew closer, Gates made no move. This hesitation was more than Arnold could bear. It maddened him that he could not act without orders from "Granny Gates." But Gates's well-known tendency to hold back was exactly what Burgoyne was counting on. He planned to come at Gates's Bemis Heights troops in three columns. His men would move in, capture, and destroy. The Americans would be pushed east to the river and made to surrender.

It might have happened that way had it not been for Arnold. His first aggressive move came on September 19, 1777. Burgoyne's troops were spotted marching a few miles north of Bemis Heights. After much pleading, Arnold finally convinced Gates to let him ride out with his men to determine how close the enemy was.

British general John Burgoyne was just 15 years old when he first entered the military.

On a broad stretch of land known as Freeman's Farm, Arnold encountered Burgoyne's men head on. A furious battle ensued while Gates and the rest of his troops remained planted back at camp. With only a few more soldiers Arnold could completely stop the British march southward. But Gates refused to send in more men. At the end of the day, the British had suffered many more losses than the patriots. But the fight was not over. Most who had fought realized that the Freeman's Farm battle could have been the decisive conflict. Gates's poor decisions had lost them the opportunity to claim a huge victory.

After the battle, soldiers and officers praised Arnold's competence and valor. Gates had done nothing to help, and many patriot lives had been lost. Many more probably would be lost, as they would be forced to fight Burgoyne again.

The high praise showered on Arnold in camp made Gates livid with resentment. He maneuvered to get credit for the battle. In his letters to friends and in his report to Congress, he did not mention Arnold's name at all. Instead, he made it appear that he had been the hero. His aides sent false accounts of the action. Their stories portrayed Arnold as the one who remained in camp.

Arnold seethed over these unrighteous acts and Gates's cowardice. They argued violently. Arnold became so enraged that Gates took away his command and gave him a pass to leave camp. But Arnold clearly sensed that he was at the site of what would be a major decisive battle. Even his wounded pride would not allow him to leave.

On the clear fall morning of October 7, 1777, Burgoyne's forces began to advance south toward Bemis Heights once again. It took Gates three hours to react, but finally he agreed to send in patriot troops. Gates remained safely at headquarters.

Although Arnold had orders to remain in camp,

he defied his commanding officer. Suddenly he appeared in the midst of combat, on horseback and dressed in his officer's uniform. He flew into battle with his sword held high.

On the field, those in command gladly let Arnold take the lead. Within seconds he assessed the situation and conceived a battle plan. Encouraged by their commander, the patriot troops surged forward, their spirits renewed.

As combat raged, Arnold rode furiously back and forth across the clearing between friendly and enemy lines. He shouted orders and encouragements to "his lads." Musket balls whizzed past his head, but none touched him. His single-minded purpose was to defeat the enemy.

Arnold provided a fearless example. Following his lead, thousands of soldiers rose to the heights of courage and heroism. By the end of the day, the outcome was clear. More than 600 redcoats had been wounded, captured, or killed. The rest were retreating. The patriots had suffered far fewer casualties.

The last focal point of the battle was Breymann's Redoubt, a small and poorly defended fortification. Just as the sun was setting, with Burgoyne's men retreating, Arnold rode into the redoubt. The few redcoats still there were so shocked by his bold entry that there was a moment of stunned silence. Then Arnold raised his sword, a signal for the charge.

Before he could attack, musket fire rang out. Arnold went down, his horse dead on top of him. The enemy got a last good shot before getting out.

The weight of his fallen horse fractured Arnold's leg in several places.

Arnold was wounded in his lower left leg, just as he had been in Quebec. As his men worked to pull him out from under his horse, he continued to shout orders until the pain silenced him. One of his loyal captains later reported that Arnold said he wished the musket ball had missed his leg and "passed his heart" instead. ✑

8 TYRANT OF PHILADELPHIA

Chapter

❦

If a musket ball had indeed pierced Arnold's heart at Breymann's Redoubt, he would have died a hero. As it was, he was alive to endure what followed.

Arnold had effectively stopped the redcoats' forward progress. After 10 days, General Burgoyne accepted the fact that he had just one option left: surrender. Gates rode with thousands of new recruits to Saratoga and accepted Burgoyne's surrender. Congress created a gold medal in Gates's honor and called him a "gallant leader."

Burgoyne himself publicly credited Arnold with his defeat. But it made no difference. Arnold's enemies made sure Gates's name became the only one associated with the battle that changed the tide of the Revolutionary War.

Shortly after surrendering his troops to General Gates in Saratoga, British general Burgoyne returned to England and resigned from the military in disgrace.

Nearly 6,000 British soldiers surrendered themselves as prisoners of war following the Battle of Saratoga.

As Gates was showered with glory, Arnold lay brooding in an Albany hospital bed. To him the "Revolution" was beginning to look like an empty cause led by visionless, self-serving fools. But he had not lost the will to fight.

Most immediately he was fighting for his own

shattered leg. Doctors insisted it must be amputated. Arnold furiously refused. To spend the rest of his life immobilized was out of the question. Instead, a bulky contraption called a fracture box was put on his leg to help it mend.

Arnold's recuperation was slow and painful. But the great frustration he felt over not being recognized for his efforts made him ornery and difficult. After five months in the hospital, he was finally well enough to go home. But he left the hospital on crutches, his left leg now 2 inches (5 centimeters) shorter than his right. He would always limp, even with a built-up heel on his shoe.

On November 29, 1777, while Arnold was still in the hospital, Congress voted to restore the seniority he had long been denied, finally moving him ahead of those major generals who'd been promoted earlier in the year. A few months later, General Washington sent Arnold a sword knot and epaulets to adorn his officer's uniform. But even these honors were small return for what Arnold had sacrificed.

For more than two years Arnold had had no family life. He had ignored his business. He had given everything to the fight for liberty, risking death many times. In return he got nothing but insults, outrageous claims against him, and injuries.

But as the new year of 1778 rolled in, Arnold outwardly seemed committed. He had signed the oath of

Until 1830, Philadelphia was the largest city in the United States.

allegiance that all officers were now required to sign, which stated: "I will to the utmost of my power support, maintain, and defend the said United States against the said King George the Third ... and will serve ... with fidelity, according to the best of my skill and understanding."

Washington still had faith in Arnold's military

abilities and looked upon him as a masterful leader, one who had been treated unjustly by Congress. He wanted to give Arnold another chance. But Arnold's leg injury kept him from being fit for active service in the army, so Washington named him the military governor of Philadelphia, Pennsylvania.

Philadelphia had been the headquarters of the British military for nine months. Now they were retreating to New York City. In June 1778, Philadelphia became Arnold's own little kingdom.

He did not get off to a good start. With Congress back in Philadelphia, Arnold had constant dealings with men he considered his enemies. He had little tact and no diplomatic skills, and he found ways to challenge, harass, and humiliate anyone who had worked against him.

Further, though the British military had fled the city, many Loyalists remained. Arnold was attracted by their wealth and class. He befriended them and began to style his life after theirs. He moved into an impressive home and rode through town in a fine horse-drawn carriage.

All the impulses that had driven Arnold's early life, including his desire for wealth and power, were coming back into play. But he could hardly keep up his extravagant lifestyle on a military salary. He was lured by questionable business deals. And soon he had fallen deeply into debt.

Within months, Arnold's uncooperative attitude and lavish living had turned many bitterly against him. His political enemies and other patriot civilians labeled him a military dictator. They claimed he abused his authority and had used military personnel and supplies for his own private benefit.

In early February 1779, Arnold's enemies issued a long public statement against him. The proclamation listed eight ways in which he had supposedly acted dishonestly or abused his power. He resigned his command and called for an immediate court martial to clear his name.

Judge Shippen at first objected to his daughter's romantic involvement with Arnold but later gave in to her wishes.

The one bright light in Arnold's life during this time was Margaret (Peggy) Shippen.

The 37-year-old captain had met 18-year-old Peggy at a Fourth of July celebration in 1778, three years after his wife's death. Peggy was the daughter of Edward Shippen, a well-respected judge in Philadelphia. Peggy was impressed by the refined style of the British, and she could not understand why anyone would give up the comforts and security of life under British rule.

Beautiful and intelligent, Peggy wanted a man who could afford her own extravagant lifestyle. She found the patriots generally crude and obnoxious. She preferred the dashing British officers who moved in the same social circles she did. Now that they were gone she had no one to flirt with or to show her affection—until she met Arnold.

Arnold was a patriot, but he was flashy and high-living. He had a prestigious military rank and was a hero as well. Peggy and Arnold married on April 8, 1779. Peggy was a comfort to Arnold in difficult times. Shortly before their marriage, he confided to her in a letter:

> *Arnold was a proud and passionate family man, despite not often being at home with his many children. With his first wife, Margaret, he had three sons. The first, Benedict VI, died a young man while in the British military. The other two settled in Canada. He also had three sons and a daughter with Peggy.*

> *I am heartily tired with my journey, and almost so with human nature. I daily discover so much baseness and ingratitude among mankind that I almost blush at being of the same species.*

Arnold's troubles continued. Frantic to be cleared of all wrongdoing, he sent letters to General Washington. He could not hide his resentment and disgust at the way he had been treated by those he had given so much to defend. Still, the inquiry into Arnold's conduct kept being delayed for one reason after another. In the end, he was found guilty of two of the eight charges. The court ruled that Arnold had violated the articles of war by allowing an enemy ship to dock in a U.S. harbor. Also, he had improperly used military wagons for his own personal gain.

But the hearing in which these decisions were made did not take place until January of 1780. As he waited anxiously through 1779 for the final verdict, Arnold's patriotic loyalty began to drain away. If he could not gain the respect he craved from his Revolutionary peers, perhaps he could get it from someone else.

In a Loyalist newspaper article Arnold had been called "an officer more distinguished for valor and perseverance than any commander in [the Continental] service." The British obviously thought more highly of him than his own government did. Further, he had heard that they were offering large sums of money to patriot officers who might want to change sides.

Arnold desperately needed money to maintain his lifestyle with Peggy and to provide for his family. He had long suffered the humiliations brought on him by his American enemies.

It made sense to him that he turn his allegiance

Arnold's second wife, Peggy, is shown here with his only daughter, Sophia Matilda.

to the British. Peggy too was fed up with a war that seemed senseless to her. She believed the Americans would never win against the powerful British forces. In her opinion, the sooner the rebellion was brought to an end the better. History shows that it was most likely Peggy, then, who first opened the door to the enemy for her husband. ✑

9 DEADLY DECEIT

Chapter

❧⟨✦⟩❧

While the British had occupied Philadelphia, Peggy had been at the center of a social whirl. Among her many admirers had been the sophisticated British major John André. Even after André left the city, Peggy remained in contact with him and likely told him of her husband's plans to defect.

General Henry Clinton had replaced General Sir William Howe as commander in chief of the British military. In New York City, Clinton appointed André as his chief intelligence officer. As such, he was in constant communication with Clinton.

Arnold's first contact with André occurred on May 9, 1779. Using a trusted Loyalist as his go-between, Arnold communicated his willingness to change sides. Neither André nor Clinton could

Benedict Arnold wrote pages of U.S. military secrets and convinced John André to carry them back to British headquarters concealed in his boots.

The first code name Arnold chose for himself was "Monk." George Monk was a 17th-century English military general. When the English Revolution fractured into small groups, Monk saw that they were incapable of running the country. He changed sides and conspired to return power to the monarchy. His mission succeeded, and he became a national hero. Arnold did not continue to use the name Monk. He later used "Gustavus" and "John Moore." John André took the name "John Anderson" and was sometimes referred to as "Lothario." Peggy Arnold's code name was "Mrs. Moore."

believe that one of America's most skilled officers was really defecting. They proceeded carefully. In his reply, André informed Arnold that if he could truly help the British, he would be richly rewarded. He established a code by which they could communicate.

Throughout the summer, the secret correspondence went on as Arnold began to provide U.S. military secrets to the British. Getting messages through enemy lines was complicated. Sometimes weeks went by before one or the other received a letter. Arnold was sending valuable information, but Clinton wanted something "big." Helping to capture West Point, a huge U.S. military complex on the Hudson River, would be a start, André hinted.

In response, Arnold asked for a guaranteed payment of 10,000 pounds—a huge amount of money at the time. To this point, his traitorous communications had never been in his own handwriting. They had gone to André by word of mouth or in another's

handwriting. There was nothing to tie Arnold to a betrayal. If suspected of spying, he could still deny everything. There would be no proof.

West Point's elevated position on the west bank of the Hudson River provided the patriots with a clear view of approaching vessels.

Now, if he were going to risk everything, Arnold wanted to get paid well. This wasn't the only reason he demanded so much. Congress had repeatedly refused to reimburse the money he had spent over the years because of his lack of receipts. In all, Arnold's losses equaled about $275,000 in modern U.S. dollars. He had a family to support and another child on the way. He was desperate for money.

As their dealings went on, distrust between André and Arnold grew. Arnold even began to talk of

British-born spy John André sailed to North America in 1774, where he quickly became a favorite in high-society circles for his artistic talents.

dropping the whole thing and rejoining the U.S. military. But Peggy disagreed. She wrote André herself and smoothed the way for negotiations to continue between the two men.

But Clinton wanted to be absolutely sure Arnold was really the one they were dealing with. André wrote Arnold to arrange a face-to-face meeting. Once they had met in person, he assured Arnold, his payment should be secure. Finally, André asked for plans of West Point and a list of all the vessels in the Hudson River near the fort itself.

Continuing to appear loyal to the United States, Arnold tried to get command of the complex. Situated on the banks of the Hudson River, West Point was critically important to the patriots. It included seven forts, which had cost millions of dollars to build. The United States could command the whole waterway as long as it had a strong military force active at West Point. If the British gained control of the fort, the rebellion would soon collapse.

Arnold made visits to West Point even before

officially becoming its commander. He passed on all the information he could gather to André.

By 1780, patriot morale was low. Loyalists were spreading the idea that successful revolution was now hopeless. Washington was fearful that many of his troops were ready to quit the fight entirely. Wanting a reliable, brave-hearted leader in command, he asked Arnold to head the entire left wing of the army. This was a position of great honor, but Arnold declined. Instead, he asked for command of West Point. Washington agreed. Now Arnold was free and clear to "sell" West Point to the enemy.

By September 1780, Arnold had moved his family into the stately Robinson house across the river from West Point. He was also finally arranging his meeting with André to discuss the details of how the fort would be surrendered. Arnold's treacherous plan also included the capture of General Washington. He knew that Washington would be returning from a meeting in Connecticut at the same time the fort was to be taken.

Arnold and André had many difficulties in getting their communications to one another. Weeks passed between letters. Impatience mounted. Their first attempt to meet failed entirely. But finally they managed to rendezvous.

In the moonless hours after midnight on Friday, September 22, a small boat crossed the Hudson

River. The boat was carrying Major André from the British ship *Vulture* to the west bank of the river several miles south of West Point. As the boat approached the shore, Arnold appeared from behind the dark fir trees. He and André disappeared into the woods, while André's escorts waited anxiously at the boat.

The meeting between the two spies lasted long into the night. The oarsmen of André's small boat had grown tired and fearful and had deserted their post. There was no one to take André back to the *Vulture*. Arnold decided to take André to the home of Samuel Hett Smith, a trusted friend. There, they could continue their conference. They slipped away to Smith's home.

Suddenly, a cannon blast reverberated in the air. Rushing to the window, André saw the *Vulture*—his getaway ship—moving south on the river. The Americans had fired on the ship. André was trapped behind enemy lines.

But Arnold had a plan. He commanded Smith to escort André overland several miles to a place where André could easily get back to his ship. He gave André six pages of information about West Point and provided him with an expensive horse. Then he wrote passes for Smith and André in case anyone stopped them on their way.

Before 10 a.m. on Friday morning, Arnold confi-

> Head Quarters Robinsons
> House Sepr. 22d. 1780
>
> Permit Mr. John Anderson to pass the
> Guards to the White Plains, or below
> if He Chuses. He being on Public
> Business by my Direction
>
> B. Arnold MGenl

Benedict Arnold signed this pass to grant John André (using the code name John Anderson) safe passage across patriot lines.

dently returned to his headquarters at the Robinson house. That evening, André slipped the papers into his boots, covered his officer's coat with a civilian cloak, and began his dangerous trip back to safety.

General Clinton had given André a few all-important orders for his meeting with Arnold: André was not to cross into the enemy's territory. If he did, he would no longer be under British protection. He was by no means to disguise himself in any way. And finally, he was ordered not to carry any papers related to the West Point plan when he returned. As he rode off, André was breaking all three orders that would ensure his safety.

10 DISCOVERY AND DOWNFALL

⸙⸙⸙

On Monday, September 25, 1780, Arnold was enjoying breakfast at home with a few of his officers when a messenger delivered a letter informing him that John André had been captured. The critical papers and the pass signed by Arnold had been discovered as well. Arnold calmly left the breakfast table and rushed upstairs to privately inform Peggy of the disaster. Returning to his guests, he made hasty excuses and fled on horseback.

Arnold made a desperate run to his private barge. There, he ordered the bargemen to take him downriver to the *Vulture*.

The officers onboard the *Vulture* were relieved to see Arnold's barge approaching. They had heard no news of André throughout the weekend. They

An artist's rendering of Benedict Arnold telling his wife, Peggy, that their deceit had been discovered

were fearful of what had happened to him. Now they believed Arnold was bringing him back safe. But seeing Arnold alone confirmed their worst fears. Though André was not with him, Arnold safely boarded the *Vulture*.

Arnold had made his desperate escape at mid-morning. By the time Washington arrived at West Point several hours later, Arnold was long gone with the British. He had not only spied and defected. He had written letters containing bold-faced lies of loyalty to General Washington, always his greatest supporter. He had plotted his commander in chief's capture.

Washington was staggered by the news. He later announced,

... treason of the blackest dye was yesterday discovered. General Arnold ... was about to ... give the American cause a deadly wound if not fatal stab ... Its [discovery] affords the most convincing proof that the Liberties of America are the object of divine Protection.

After Arnold fled, Peggy staged a false hysterical fit. Her posture as the innocent wife fully convinced the patriots. They pitied her as a pawn in the plot of her greedy, self-serving husband. It was years after her death that Americans discovered her active role in the betrayal. But the British officers had known all along. Before the Arnolds left New York, King George III awarded Peggy a royal pension of 500 pounds. The pension was a result of General Clinton's petition on her behalf, for her "very meritorious" services in the plan to take West Point.

After a court hearing the following weekend, André was condemned to death by hanging. Many letters were written pleading with Washington to spare him. Even Arnold had the nerve to write on André's behalf. Courageous and calm to the very last, André was hung at noon on Monday, October 5, 1780.

Although he asked to be shot, which was considered a "gentlemanly" way to die, rather than hung, John André nevertheless met his end on the gallows.

Arnold had believed that American resistance was weakening. His attempt to deliver West Point was based on that belief. For once, his risky behavior had not paid off. News of Arnold's betrayal sent a surge of patriotic fervor through the new country. Everywhere in American towns and villages, Arnold's effigy was variously hung, burned, or mutilated by outraged crowds. His betrayal had brought a powerful unity of purpose to Americans in a way that nothing else could have.

André was gone. But General Clinton believed Arnold would greatly strengthen his army and inspire other American officers to cross over to the British side. Arnold thought so, too.

Both were completely wrong. Arnold offered gold, uniforms, equipment, and permanent positions

Angry Americans portrayed Benedict Arnold as two-faced and in league with the devil for his role as a spy.

in the British military to any patriot who would join him. Only about 200 men accepted the offer.

Arnold was appointed a colonel in the permanent British military. In combat against the Americans, he served as a brigadier general. He was generously compensated for what he had lost by becoming a Loyalist.

Although he was a wanted criminal in the United States, Arnold did not set sail immediately for England. In January 1781, he led British forces in raiding the city of Richmond, Virginia. Enraged, Virginia governor Thomas Jefferson offered the handsome reward of 5,000 guineas to anyone who could capture Arnold. No one succeeded.

In September of the same year, Clinton sent Arnold to capture New London, Connecticut. New London was an important rebel ammunition depot a few miles from Arnold's hometown of Norwich. Arnold was back in the territory where he had suffered his first humiliations and disgrace.

The raid against New London was bloody and extreme. Arnold burned military targets, homes, and stores. Many people were killed. Another officer raided nearby Fort Griswold. There, many American soldiers were slaughtered, even after they had surrendered. With this last furious act against his former countrymen, Arnold became the most despised American ever. ℘

11 AFTER THE FALL

❧❧❧

In December 1781, Arnold and his family sailed for London, England. But Arnold did not settle into a retired man's life. His thirst for revenge against the patriots was not satisfied.

Britain's General Cornwallis had surrendered to General Washington on October 19, 1781, at Yorktown, Virginia. To nearly everyone on both sides, this had signaled the end of the war. But Arnold still believed he could lead the British troops in a final destruction of American rebellion.

In the United States, Arnold had gained the respect of many British officers. Once in London, he presented battle plans to many influential people, who at first took him seriously. For a while the Arnold family enjoyed the favor of King George III. But the

General Washington and his troops were aided by French and Native American allies to force the British to surrender in Yorktown in 1781.

tide turned when the Tories lost political control to the Whigs. The more liberal Whig party was strongly anti-war. The Whigs were tired of the fight against the United States. They supported American independence and had little respect for the ex-patriot traitor.

Not seeing the possibility of action, Arnold retired as a colonel that same year. But he could not give up his dream of wealth and glory.

Through the 1780s and into the 1790s, Arnold focused on business ventures. In 1785, he moved his family to Saint John in Nova Scotia, Canada. He speculated in real estate, bought a fleet of ships, and for a while prospered as a merchant. He spent freely

One-tenth of England's entire population lived in London by 1750.

and just as freely loaned money and gave credit where it was needed. But he was never well accepted in Saint John, even by the Loyalists. In 1792, the Arnolds returned to London.

In London, Arnold turned back to the sea and began trading in the West Indies. Riding the waves on his own ship gave him the contentment he lacked everywhere else. But 1793 marked the beginning of the Reign of Terror (a period during the French Revolution) in France, which led to another war with England. Arnold tried again to win a military commission, this time to fight in the Caribbean. When that failed, he outfitted his own ship to attack the French and sent useful intelligence back to the British. Again, he was highly praised by those men who fought with him.

Even at 53, Arnold had not lost his impulse for adventure. In 1794, the French captured him in

While in Nova Scotia, Arnold hired a laborer to help at his wharf. Though Arnold did not recognize him, the man, John Shackford, knew Arnold well. He had served under Arnold during the march through the Maine wilderness. Now Arnold directed Shackford again, this time to load one of his ships. Years later Shackford wrote about that day, "… I sat upon the ship's deck [to] watch the movements of my old commander who had carried us through everything, and for whose skill and courage I retained my former admiration, despite his treason. But when I thought of what he had been and the despised man he then was, tears would come and I could not help it."

Guadeloupe—a pair of islands in the West Indies—and threw him into a prison cell onboard a French ship. When he learned that he was about to be beheaded, Arnold bribed a guard and escaped through a portal, dropping into a small boat waiting in the waters below.

Arnold had remained healthy and vigorous throughout the 1790s. But by the end of that decade many physical ailments plagued him. He had a persistent cough. His gout had returned with a vengeance, swelling his legs so that he could not walk. He had difficulty breathing because of asthma. Back in London, in the early morning hours of June 14, 1801, Arnold passed away in his sleep. He was 60 years old.

It is difficult to know for sure who Benedict Arnold really was or to understand the intense impulses that drove him. But his story is essentially a tragedy. His life took him soaring to the heights then plunged him down again—repeatedly. His controversial personality won him loyal friends and made bitter foes. He longed to be recognized for valiant deeds. He had hoped to provide generously for his family and live in luxury. None of these things had occurred. By the end of his life, Arnold's deep flaws and insecurities had plunged him down a final time. Instead of fame he found infamy.

Arnold's subdued funeral parade through the

streets of London included seven mourning coaches and four state carriages. He was buried in St. Mary's church cemetery in the London suburb of Battersea. At the time of his burial a clerk entered Arnold's name incorrectly in the records. When the church was remodeled a century later, the cemetery was dug up, and the bodies were reburied in a mass unmarked grave. With no marker left to remember him, Benedict Arnold—hero, traitor, swashbuckling officer, husband and father, belligerent foe, daredevil kid—would be forgotten for many years to come. ∾

Despite his early acts of heroism, Benedict Arnold will always be remembered for his betrayal.

ARNOLD'S LIFE

1755

Begins his apprentice-
ship in Norwich

1741

Benedict Arnold V
is born in Norwich,
Connecticut

1762

Moves to
New London
to open his
own business

1740

1756–63

The Seven Years' War
is fought; Britain
defeats France

1741

Germany's Handel
composes his
Messiah

WORLD EVENTS

1775

Raids Fort Ticonderoga with
Ethan Allen; later leads the
march through the Maine
wilderness to Canada; his
wife, Margaret, dies

1776

Leads the battle
against the British
at Valcour Island

1767

Marries Margaret
Mansfield

1770

1775

English novelist Jane
Austen born

1769

British explorer
Captain James Cook
reaches New Zealand

ARNOLD'S LIFE

1779

Marries Peggy Shippen; begins his secret correspondence with British major John André

1777

Helps defeat the British at Freeman's Farm, leading to Burgoyne's surrender at Saratoga

1778

Goes to Philadelphia as military governor

1778

British explorer Captain James Cook explores the Hawaiian Islands

1779

Jan Ingenhousz of the Netherlands discovers that plants release oxygen when exposed to sunlight

WORLD EVENTS

1780

Flees West Point and
joins the British army
after André is captured as
a spy by the Americans;
is labeled a traitor

1781

Leads the British raid on
New London, Connecticut;
later sails with his family
to London, England

1783

Britain and the
United States
sign a peace
treaty

1780

1783

American author
Washington Irving is
born

Joseph Michel and
Jacques Étienne
Montgolfier became the
first human beings to fly
with their invention of
the hot-air balloon

ARNOLD'S LIFE

1791

The Arnold family
returns to London

1785

Moves his family to
Nova Scotia, Canada;
later sails to Jamaica to
try to build his new
business

1794

Sails to the West Indies,
where he is captured by
the French but later
escapes

1790

1791

Austrian composer
Wolfgang Amadeus
Mozart dies

1786

The British government
announces its plans to
make Australia a penal
colony

WORLD EVENTS

1796–1800

Tries repeatedly to get another military commission with the British army but has no success

1795

Returns to England and his family

1801

Dies in London on June 14

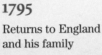

1800

1799

Napoleon Bonaparte takes control of France

The Rosetta stone, which was the key to understanding Egyptian hieroglyphics, is found near Rosetta, Egypt

1801

Ultraviolet radiation is discovered

DATE OF BIRTH: January 14, 1741

BIRTHPLACE: Norwich, Connecticut

FATHER: Benedict Arnold IV
(c. 1715–1761)

MOTHER: Hannah Waterman King
Arnold (1706–1759)

EDUCATION: Private academy in
Canterbury, Connecticut

FIRST SPOUSE: Margaret Mansfield
(c. 1745–1775)

DATE OF MARRIAGE: February 27, 1767

CHILDREN: Benedict VI (1768–1795);
Richard (1769–1847);
Henry (1772–1826)

SECOND SPOUSE: Margaret "Peggy" Shippen
Arnold (1760–1804)

DATE OF MARRIAGE: April 8, 1779

CHILDREN: Edward (1780–1813);
James (1781–1854);
Sophia (1785–1828);
George (1787–1828);
William (c. 1794–1846)

DATE OF DEATH: June 14, 1801

PLACE OF BURIAL: Battersea, England, a
suburb of London

In the Library

Gaines, Ann Graham. *Benedict Arnold: Patriot or Traitor?* (Historical American Biographies). Berkeley Heights, N.J.: Enslow Publishers, 2001.

Gregson, Susan R. *Benedict Arnold* (Let Freedom Ring: American Revolution Biographies). Mankato, Minn.: Capstone Press, 2001.

Hossell, Karen Price. *Benedict Arnold* (American War Biographies). St. Louis, Mo.: Heinemann Library, 2004.

King, David C. *Benedict Arnold and the American Revolution*. San Diego: Blackbirch Press, 1998.

Worth, Richard. *Saratoga* (Battles That Changed the World). Langhorne, Pa.: Chelsea House, 2002.

On the Web

For more information on *Benedict Arnold*, use FactHound to track down Web sites related to this book.

1. Go to *www.facthound.com*
2. Type in a search word related to this book or this book ID: 0756508258
3. Click on the *Fetch It* button.

FactHound will find the best Web sites for you.

Historic Sites

International Spy Museum
800 F Street NW
Washington, D.C. 20004
202/393-7798
A museum devoted to the role spies have played worldwide throughout history

Saratoga National Historical Park
648 Route 32
Stillwater, N.Y. 12170-1604
518/664-9821, ext. 224
Site of the Battles of Saratoga in 1777; features a monument to the heroic acts and wounding of Benedict Arnold

allies
groups, such as countries, favorably associated with one another by treaty or agreement

apothecary
a shopkeeper who prepares and sells medicinal herbs and remedies

apprenticeships
stated amounts of time during which people are legally bound to learn a trade or an art from others who are experienced in that field

arsenal
a storehouse or collection of weapons

bail
to pay money for the temporary release of a prisoner from jail

effigy
a rough or crude figure constructed to represent a hated person

epaulets
ornamental fringed shoulder pads or loops worn as part of a military uniform

guineas
English gold coins

infamy
the reputation of being the worst kind of criminal or evil-doer

Loyalist
one who is loyal to the British throne

militia
a body of citizens organized for military service

muskets
guns with long barrels used before rifles were invented

reconciliation
a return to peace

redcoats
another name for British soldiers

redoubt
a small, usually temporary enclosed defensive structure

regiment
a military group

rendezvous
to meet at a prearranged place and time

siege
a military attack or blockade upon a city or fortress to force its surrender

turncoat
someone who switches to another party or changes loyalties to another side

vessel
a watercraft bigger than a rowboat; a ship

Whigs
members of the British political party that was opposed to the Tories

Chapter 2

Page 17, line 14: Willard Sterne Randall. *Benedict Arnold: Patriot and Traitor.* New York: William Morrow and Company, 1990, p. 24.

Page 17, line 22: Clare Brandt. *The Man in the Mirror: A Life of Benedict Arnold.* New York: Random House, 1994, p. 5.

Chapter 3

Page 31, line 3: *Benedict Arnold: Patriot and Traitor* (Randall), p. 78.

Page 33, line 10: James Kirby Martin. *Benedict Arnold, Revolutionary Hero: An American Warrior Reconsidered.* New York: New York University Press, 1997, p.63.

Chapter 6

Page 57, sidebar: Ibid., p. 324.

Chapter 8

Page 70, line 2: Jean Fritz. *Traitor: The Case of Benedict Arnold.* New York: Putnam's Sons, 1981, p. 99.

Page 73, line 20: *Benedict Arnold, Revolutionary Hero: An American Warrior Reconsidered* (Martin), p. 428.

Page 74, line 17: *The Man in the Mirror: A Life of Benedict Arnold* (Brandt), p. 172.

Chapter 10

Page 86, line 19: Bill Federer. "The American Minute: August 30." *Center for Christian Statesmanship.* http://www.statesman.org/AmericanMinute.asp?date=8/30&year

Blanco, Richard L., ed. *The American Revolution 1775–1783, An Encyclopedia, Vol. 1.* New York: Garland Publishing, 1993.

Boylan, Brian Richard. *Benedict Arnold: The Dark Eagle.* New York: W. W. Norton & Company, 1973.

Brandt, Clare. *The Man in the Mirror: A Life of Benedict Arnold.* New York: Random House, 1994.

Decker, Malcolm. *Ten Days of Infamy: An Illustrated Memoir of the Arnold-Andre Conspiracy.* New York: Arno Press, 1969.

Fritz, Jean. *Traitor: The Case of Benedict Arnold.* New York: G. P. Putnam's Sons, 1981.

Johnson, Allen, ed. *Dictionary of American Biography, Vol. 1.* New York: Charles Scribner's Sons, 1964.

Lengyel, Cornel. *I, Benedict Arnold: The Anatomy of Treason.* Garden City, N.Y.: Doubleday & Company, 1960.

Martin, James Kirby. *Benedict Arnold, Revolutionary Hero: An American Warrior Reconsidered.* New York: New York University Press, 1997.

Randall, Willard Sterne. *Benedict Arnold: Patriot and Traitor.* New York: William Morrow and Company, 1990.

Sale, Richard. *The Worst Acts of Treason in American History: From Benedict Arnold to Robert Hanssen.* New York: Berkeley Publishing Group, 2003.

Wilson, Barry K. *Benedict Arnold: A Traitor in Our Midst.* Montreal: McGill-Queen's University Press, 2001.

Wood, W. J. *Battles of the Revolutionary War, 1775–1781.* New York: De Capo Press, 1995.

Pamela Dell was born in Idaho, grew up in Chicago, and now lives in southern California. She began her career writing for adults and started writing for children about 12 years ago. Since then she has published fiction and nonfiction books, written numerous magazine articles, and created award-winning interactive multimedia. Among many other things, Pamela loves technology, the Internet, books, movies, curious people, and cats, especially black cats.

Image Credits